Little RIDDLERS

Leicestershire

Edited By Jenni Harrison

First published in Great Britain in 2018 by:

YoungWriters

Young Writers
Remus House
Coltsfoot Drive
Peterborough
PE2 9BF
Telephone: 01733 890066
Website: www.youngwriters.co.uk

FOREWORD

Dear Reader,
Are you ready to get your thinking caps on to puzzle
your way through this wonderful collection?

Young Writers' Little Riddlers competition set out to
encourage young writers to create their own riddles.
Their answers could be whatever or whoever their
imaginations desired; from people to places, animals
to objects, food to seasons. Riddles are a great way
to further the children's use of poetic expression,
including onomatopoeia and similes, as well as
encourage them to 'think outside the box' by
providing clues without giving the answer away
immediately.

All of us here at Young Writers believe in the
importance of inspiring young children to produce
creative writing, including poetry, and we feel that
seeing their own riddles in print will keep that
creative spirit burning brightly and proudly.

We hope you enjoy riddling your way through this
book as much as we enjoyed reading all the entries.

CONTENTS

Sebastian Goddard (7)	64
Mollie Edwards (5)	65
Maisie Howett (7)	66
Evie Hunt (6)	67
Reuben Hill (6)	68
Josie Brant (6)	69
Teddie Atkins (5)	70
Matilda Wright (6)	71
Max Shilton (6)	72
Alexandra Dowling (6)	73
Isla Blossom Paragreen (6)	74
Isabel Lewington (6)	75
Daniel John Bettles (6)	76
Isaac Lawrence (6)	77
Archie Underwood (5)	78
Isla Sammels (5)	79
Austin Toby Worth (6)	80
Imogen Ellen Worth (5)	81
Jessica Burniston (5)	82
Luna Stevenson (6)	83
Kallum Beacham (5)	84
Thomas Hollins (6)	85
Stanley Tyers (6)	86
Ruby Thompson (6)	87
Jessica-Lily Jones (6)	88
Sophie Fox (6)	89
Darcie Booton (5)	90
Jude Clift (6)	91
Freddie Shilcock (6)	92
Taiyon Rhamell James Henry (6)	93
Lucas Young (6)	94
Lily Rose Illston-Hughes (5)	95
Harry James Butler (6)	96
Isobel Richardson (5)	97
Liam Blackett (6)	98
James Toon (6)	99
Giovanni Backus (5)	100
India Griffiths-Brown (6)	101
Hiro Vine Peake (5)	102
Dean Beacham (5)	103

Leicester International School, Leicester

Saeed Nurmamade (6)	104
Fatemah Esat (6)	105

Manor House School, Ashby-De-La-Zouch

Deep Desai (5)	106
Samuel Gobey (5)	107
Zara Esat (6)	108
Charlie Simon Dunn (6)	109
Christopher Cheneler (6)	110

Marriott Primary School, Leicester

Lexi-Rae Jordan-Summer (6)	111
Alfie Shenton (7)	112
Beau Noon (7)	113
Jack David Briers (7)	114
Ifunanya Sophia Mbolu (7)	115
Nevaeh Feral (7)	116
Sarah Pegararo (7)	117
Mia Alyssia Mayers (6)	118
Jacek Machajewski (7)	119
Tyler West (7)	120
Nicole Serwaa Antwi (7)	121
Iyvvorie Smith (7)	122
Casey Crewe (7)	123

Shenton Primary School, Leicester

Juned Mulla (6)	124
Khadijha Yusuf (6)	125
Darpan Barad (7)	126
Bilal Sajid (8)	127
Rashan Al-Jaf (7)	128
Navya Bharat Kumar (8)	129
Abdulaziz Fadra (6)	130
Joy Patel (7)	131
Abdirahman Iraad Saleeman (7)	132
Noelkanth Naresh (7)	133

THE POEMS

Colourful Stripes

I am as bright as the sun.
I have lots of different colours.
I love the sun and lots of rain.
You can see me in the blue sky.
You might find a beautiful gold pot.
I twinkle so bright.
What am I?

Answer: A rainbow.

Katie Hayes (6)
Brookside Primary School, East Leake

What Am I?

I have two big eyes.
I have a long tail and four legs.
I have lots of whiskers.
I like to go outside.
You see my eyes in the middle of the street.
I have babies called kittens.
What am I?

Answer: A cat.

Francesca Eden Peace Calladine (6)
Brookside Primary School, East Leake

The Green Hopper

I can be very poisonous.
I am usually slimy and green.
I can live in your flowery garden.
I can also live in the dark forests.
I eat raw flies.
I jump on green lily pads.
What am I?

Answer: A frog.

Millie Grace Franklin (7)
Brookside Primary School, East Leake

Fat Animal

I am very fat and big.
I'm grey.
I have four legs and a very short tail.
I am quite slow.
I have very big, humongous feet.
I have a very long trunk.
What am I?

Answer: An elephant.

Ethan Philip Furness (6)
Brookside Primary School, East Leake

Sea Animals

I have two small, black, beady eyes.
I love to eat tasty fish.
I have long, thin whiskers.
I like cold places.
I live in the sea.
I have grey skin.
What am I?

Answer: A seal.

Ellie Shannon Scott (7)
Brookside Primary School, East Leake

Footless Fun

I rise to the top slowly
and quickly come down.

At the top I see only white,
no footprints can be found
Only tracks in the light
and the wind is the only sound.

Sometimes bumpy, sometimes smooth,
the surface really makes me move.
I look so cool in my purple gear,
I only do this once a year.

My reward is a medal and a hot chocolate
and now I feel warm again inside.
Or is it the pride,
that I stayed upright?

I must stop writing now
and plan my next visit.
You can come too,
if you guess it!
What am I?

Answer: A skier.

Órla Leokadia Monica Gorman (7)
Greenfield Primary School, Countesthorpe

The Big City

Big Ben lives here
and the Queen lives very near.
Lots of people visit me,
I have an M&M shop for you to see.
I have a big river through my middle,
about this city I write this riddle.
I have a big wheel called The Eye,
where you can watch the city go by.
At my tower I had a fire,
the flames grew higher and higher.
Where am I?

Answer: London.

Ollie Boswell (6)
Greenfield Primary School, Countesthorpe

The Wizard

I have a scar on my head.
I wear glasses too.
My favourite sport is quidditch.
When I play I go as fast as a cheetah.
I have two friends called Hermione and Ron.
We are in Gryffindor house.
When we play quidditch,
We chant "Roar, roar, Gryffindor."
On the Express we go to school,
Hogwarts is its name.
Who am I?

Answer: Harry Potter.

Thomas Berry (7)
Greenfield Primary School, Countesthorpe

Crispy Humans

I am big and scary
and sometimes friendly.
With wings that are so strong,
jump on my back and hold on tight.
My breath's hot like the sun.
My tail is long.
My teeth are as sharp as a knife.
My eyes can light up the dark.
My favourite food is burnt, crispy humans
and I often visit you in your dreams.
What am I?

Answer: A dragon.

Tallulah Astill (7)
Greenfield Primary School, Countesthorpe

The Clickers

I was born in Denmark a long time ago.
I am nice to touch
except when you stand on me with your toe.
I am made out of plastic.
You can make me into anything,
it's so fantastic!
In lots of different colours
I can be found
and when you put two of me together
you hear a clicking sound.
What am I?

Answer: Lego.

Dexter Jack Stewart (7)
Greenfield Primary School, Countesthorpe

Catch Me If You Dare!

I have brown and grey, scaly skin.
I always want to win.
I am big, scary and fierce.
I have sharp teeth that pierce.
Anyone that is near
will scream with fear.
I have razor-sharp claws.
When I am here nobody snores.
There is one thing for sure,
if you get in my way I will roar!
What am I?

Answer: A T-rex.

William Morris (6)
Greenfield Primary School, Countesthorpe

Party Nibble

I come out once a year.
I then hear a big, loud cheer.
I come in colours bold and bright.
I'm ready for you to take a bite.
I'm only lit a little bit
and when you blow me out I hear a shout.
First I'm sweet, creamy and yummy,
I then get in your tummy.
What am I?

Answer: A birthday cake.

Lillie Brewster (7)
Greenfield Primary School, Countesthorpe

Array

When you're fast asleep I come out to play.
I like to grunt and squeal.
When it gets cold I like a long sleep.
I like to eat worms,
snails and wiggly bugs.
When I'm afraid I curl up into a ball
to protect myself.
To make me look scary I have prickly spines.
What am I?

Answer: A hedgehog.

Isaac Lawrence (6)
Greenfield Primary School, Countesthorpe

Mega Builder

You can build with me.
You can stick me together without glue.
I come in lots of colours
including red, green and blue.
I get your imagination running wild.
I have a land of my own
which is fun for a child.
You can play with my people.
You can watch me in a film.
What am I?

Answer: Lego.

Hannah Nicole Parsons (6)
Greenfield Primary School, Countesthorpe

Roald Dahl

My favourite book character
is smart and pretty.
She loves to read books
and has a kind heart.
Her parents are mean
but that doesn't stop her dream.
Her teacher is sweet, kind and caring.
However her headmistress is grumpy
and doesn't like sharing.
Who is she?

Answer: Matilda.

Arabella Olivia Ruby Morris (7)
Greenfield Primary School, Countesthorpe

Catch Me If You Can

There are 25,000 species of me.
I come in all different sizes.
I was here long before dinosaurs.
I am part of one of the oldest families
to live on Earth.
I come in all different colours.
You can find me in the sea.
I can be served with chips.
Can you guess what I am?

Answer: A fish.

Miley Grace Dalton (6)
Greenfield Primary School, Countesthorpe

My Jumping Friend

I am as fluffy as a feather.
My ears stand tall just like Big Ben.
I might be small but I have a loud bark.
My tail likes to swish from side to side.
I like to say "I love you".
My eyes are as dark as the night.
I can jump very high.
What am I?

Answer: A dog.

Sophia Holland (6)
Greenfield Primary School, Countesthorpe

The Garden Predator

I live in a beloved home.
I'm cuddly, sweet and of course, adorable.
My favourite food is tuna
and I really don't like getting wet.
I make a noise that begins
with the letter 'm'
and ends with the letter 'w'.
What am I?

Answer: A cat.

Amelia Blackwell (6)
Greenfield Primary School, Countesthorpe

Squeaker

I am small, furry and cute.
My home is a big cage.
I love eating grass in the garden.
I eat hay and carrots.
I am friendly and like to be stroked.
I also like to nibble fingers.
I squeak when my food is being chopped up.
What am I?

Answer: A guinea pig.

Elliott Veitch (6)
Greenfield Primary School, Countesthorpe

Eyes Up High!

I am a mammal.
I am also a herbivore.
My babies are calves.
My ears are brown, cream and pointy.
My natural habitat is the open woodlands
and the savannah desert.
My neck is that long I can see above trees.
What am I?

Answer: A giraffe.

Imogen Norman (7)
Greenfield Primary School, Countesthorpe

Shine Bright

I am shiny but I am not gold.
I am sparkly but I'm not a diamond.
I twinkle but I am not an eye.
I can sit on your Christmas tree.
The older I get the bigger I become.
I am seen at night but I am not the moon.
What am I?

Answer: A star.

Morgan Copson (6)
Greenfield Primary School, Countesthorpe

Slippy Slider

I am black and white.
I have wings but I cannot fly.
I like to dive into the sea.
To catch my yummy tea.
I slip and slide on ice and snow.
I have a beak and I squawk and squeak.
I live where it is cold.
What am I?

Answer: A penguin.

Emily Wells (7)
Greenfield Primary School, Countesthorpe

Hard Back

I wake up when it's warm
and go to sleep when it's cold.
I like to roam the garden
eating grass and weeds.
When it is a sunny day
I like to sit and bask
with the shell that I carry on my back.
What am I?

Answer: A tortoise.

Tallulah Wood (5)
Greenfield Primary School, Countesthorpe

24

Electric Bird

I fly like a bird but I'm not alive.
I see things but I have no eyes.
I move how you tell me to.
I can't survive without batteries.
I can do loop-the-loops.
You have to have a lot of money to get me.
What am I?

Answer: A drone.

Sebastian Lowe (7)
Greenfield Primary School, Countesthorpe

The Wood That Comes To Life

I'm tall, knobbly and lean,
I have a leaf from my head that is green.
I'm brown like a stick,
I have a house that's not brick.
I live in a tree,
I have five in my family.
Who am I?

Answer: I'm Stick Man, that's me!

Hermione O'Neill (6)
Greenfield Primary School, Countesthorpe

A City Ablaze

I started in Thomas' bakery.
Songs have been sung about me.
I have hot flames like the sun.
A burning city is no fun.
I burnt houses in the past.
In Pudding Lane I spread so fast.
What am I?

Answer: The Great Fire of London.

Chloe Pallett (6)
Greenfield Primary School, Countesthorpe

Clip, Clop, Clip, Clop

I have a long mane and a swishy tail.
I like to gallop fast through the wavy grass.
I like to crunch on carrots
and nice juicy apples.
When I trot my hooves
go *clip, clip, clip, clop.*
Who am I?

Answer: Diddy the pony.

Maisie Lucas (6)
Greenfield Primary School, Countesthorpe

All Aboard

I am big and strong.
I pull coaches or trucks along.
I have a whistle or a horn,
so that I can warn.
I have wheels and piston rods.
Coal, water and fuel make me go.
I can move fast or slow.
What am I?

Answer: A train.

Luca Sturgess (6)

Greenfield Primary School, Countesthorpe

Spring

I have a very furry, white tummy.
I have a tail a little bit like scissors.
I fly away in the winter
and then I come back every spring.
I like Africa the most.
I like to be a lovely singer.
What am I?

Answer: A swallow.

Orestis Georgakis (6)
Greenfield Primary School, Countesthorpe

Fast As Lightning

I am like a huge bird.
I have steep steps.
I sit and wait for you to arrive.
I have comfy seats and a TV.
You can have your dinner on me
and have a little sleep.
I go really fast.
What am I?

Answer: An aeroplane.

Lola Rennocks (6)

Greenfield Primary School, Countesthorpe

Humongous

I am big, grey and hairy.
I am very heavy.
You wouldn't want me to sit on your knee.
I could squash your car or I could wash it!
I am very fast.
And remember... I don't forget!
What am I?

Answer: An elephant.

Oliver Louch (6)
Greenfield Primary School, Countesthorpe

I Have A Tail

I have a tail.
I like fish.
I can bite.
I make a purry song when I am happy.
I can't swim.
I like dogs.
I have a smile.
I have feet.
I have paws.
I can scratch.
What am I?

Answer: A cat.

Lilly-May Young (5)
Greenfield Primary School, Countesthorpe

Slowly Does It

I eat with my beak
and can sleep for many weeks.
I take life at a steady pace
and bask in a warm place.
My food is leafy green.
I am the hardest animal
you have ever seen.
What am I?

Answer: A tortoise.

Amelia Grace Coleman (6)
Greenfield Primary School, Countesthorpe

Can You Spot What I Am?

I am really fast.
The fastest of all.
I live in Africa
and I hide in grass that is tall.
I am the opposite of a snail.
I am the speediest in Africa.
Don't play with me!
What am I?

Answer: A cheetah.

Jasmine Hall (7)
Greenfield Primary School, Countesthorpe

The Sparkly Gold Thing

It lives in a watering can.
It's small and thin.
It can fly high where the birds can sing.
It can swing on a leaf or fly with a bee.
A part of it is sparkly for all to see.
What is it?

Answer: A golden fairy.

Lilly-Mae Kerridge (7)
Greenfield Primary School, Countesthorpe

The Beautiful Trumpet

People like to smell me.
Others like to pick me.
I am normally yellow and bright.
I represent spring.
When I appear, "Yippee," they shout.
I can brighten up a room.
What am I?

Answer: A daffodil.

Neave Haines (7)
Greenfield Primary School, Countesthorpe

Rolling Along

I come in different colours.
I can go fast or slow.
You can do tricks on me.
You can ride on me
and you can fall off me.
You have to stand on me.
I can go on ramps.
What am I?

Answer: A skateboard.

Santino Fasulo (7)
Greenfield Primary School, Countesthorpe

The Soaring Reptile

I lived a long time ago.
I could fly but I had no feathers.
I was a reptile with sharp teeth.
I had one finger but no hands.
My head had a skull crest.
I loved fish.
What am I?

Answer: A pterodactyl.

Ayden Roper (7)
Greenfield Primary School, Countesthorpe

She Is...

She is beautiful.
She is nice.
She is kind.
She cares for me.
She is mine.
She buys me toys.
She buys me sweets but not too many.
I love her and she loves me.
Who is she?

Answer: My mum.

Brodie Marc Sean Walsh (6)
Greenfield Primary School, Countesthorpe

In A Tangle

I have lots of teeth
but have no mouth and cannot eat.
I come in lots of colours.
I've got lots of style.
Sometimes I glide through.
Sometimes I get in a tangle.
What am I?

Answer: A comb.

Madison Akroyd (6)
Greenfield Primary School, Countesthorpe

Banana

I like bananas.
I'm in lots of stories.
I'm very clever.
I am an animal.
I say 'ooo aaa'.
I swing from tree to tree.
I blend in with a tree.
What am I?

Answer: A monkey.

Jessica Eales (5)
Greenfield Primary School, Countesthorpe

Roll With It

I have wheels.
The wheels can be in line.
The wheels on me can flash.
I can be any colour.
I can be tricky to start with.
You can wear me to a roller disco.
What am I?

Answer: Roller skates.

Isobel Richardson (5)
Greenfield Primary School, Countesthorpe

Kick

People can kick me.
People can boot me in goals.
I am the same shape as the world.
People can play catch with me.
People can throw me.
You have me in a match.
What am I?

Answer: A football.

Samuel Ife (5)
Greenfield Primary School, Countesthorpe

Spiky

I can be big or small.
I can be green.
I don't need much water.
I look quite mean.
You don't want to touch me.
I can be smooth or bumpy.
Can you guess what I am?

Answer: A cactus.

Francesca Dear (6)
Greenfield Primary School, Countesthorpe

Kicked

I have spots and get kicked around.
I get wet sometimes.
Players try and get me into the goal.
You can save me.
I fly through the air.
Keep your eye on me.
What am I?

Answer: A football.

Evan Griffiths-Brown (6)
Greenfield Primary School, Countesthorpe

A Purr And A Roar!

I live in the wild
but also in a house.
I stay out all night
to hunt a mouse.
I have a long tail
and I'm covered in fur.
When I'm happy I purr.
What am I?

Answer: A cat.

Georgia-Mae June Baker (7)
Greenfield Primary School, Countesthorpe

A Fishy Tale

I like to swim around.
I live in the ocean.
Disney have made a film about me.
I have a fishy tail.
My hair is really long.
I am half fish and half lady.
What am I?

Answer: A mermaid.

Isla Sammels (5)
Greenfield Primary School, Countesthorpe

Always And Forever

You cuddle me when I feel sick.
You are kind to me when others are not.
You make me feel happy when I am sad.
You teach me what's right and what's not.
Who are you?

Answer: My family.

Elyssa Diya Farmah (6)
Greenfield Primary School, Countesthorpe

Flyer

I am used on windy days.
People get me stuck in trees.
You play with me in a big field.
I am different colours.
I fly.
You can have a lot of fun with me.
What am I?

Answer: A kite.

Ella Grace Aleathea Bonner (6)
Greenfield Primary School, Countesthorpe

Multicoloured

I am shaped like an arc.
I am bright.
You can see me but not feel me.
I am usually far away.
You can see me when it's wet.
I come in many colours.
What am I?

Answer: A rainbow.

Alex Denton-Kamuti (7)
Greenfield Primary School, Countesthorpe

Pop Pop

I am sometimes white and grey.
You put bread in me.
I have levers on me.
I have turning things with numbers.
I have buttons which you press.
I pop up.
What am I?

Answer: A toaster.

Charis Barford (7)
Greenfield Primary School, Countesthorpe

52

Sophie's Roaring Riddle

I am a meat eater.
I lived a long time ago.
I am very big.
I stand on two feet.
I have sharp teeth.
I am covered in scales.
I have a long tail.
What am I?

Answer: A T-rex.

Sophie Cramp (6)
Greenfield Primary School, Countesthorpe

The Story Of My Cat

I have two pointed ears.
I have a mouthful of sharp teeth.
I have stripes along my body.
I hunt for my prey.
I like to sleep a lot.
I like fish.
What am I?

Answer: A cat.

Florence Milner (6)

Greenfield Primary School, Countesthorpe

Capital

I'm the beginning of eternity
and the end of PE.
I have four lines.
I'm after dye.
It's half of me.
I'm right of a compass.
Who am I?

Answer: E.

Edison Mitchell (7)
Greenfield Primary School, Countesthorpe

Slither

I have a long tail.
I have a long tongue.
I have spots on me.
I like it in the jungle.
I live in a log pile house.
I have a scaly skin.
What am I?

Answer: A snake.

Lilly Mason (6)
Greenfield Primary School, Countesthorpe

Roll

I have spots on me.
I am a cube.
I roll when you play games.
I have faces.
I am made up of squares.
I decide whether you win or lose.
What am I?

Answer: A dice.

Ella-Rose Young (5)
Greenfield Primary School, Countesthorpe

In The Classroom

You can draw with me.
I am a little bit long.
I can be yellow and black.
You can rub me out with a rubber.
I'm made out of wood.
What am I?

Answer: A pencil.

Isla Grace Kelsey (6)
Greenfield Primary School, Countesthorpe

Bushy Tail

I have a black nose.
I am sly.
I can sniff.
I can sweep with my tail.
I come out at night-time.
Keep your chickens locked up!
What am I?

Answer: A fox.

Benjamin Phillips (5)
Greenfield Primary School, Countesthorpe

Snappy Riddle

I have a long body.
I have a long tail.
I have snappy teeth.
I live in water.
I lay eggs.
I would eat you for dinner.
What am I?

Answer: A crocodile.

Olivia Marie Howarth (6)
Greenfield Primary School, Countesthorpe

Woof

I am very cute.
I like to jump up.
I sometimes eat shoes.
I like to do lots of tricks.
I am very furry.
I go woof, woof.
What am I?

Answer: A puppy.

Megan Sparrow (6)
Greenfield Primary School, Countesthorpe

Magical

I am not real.
I have a horn.
I exist in stories.
I have wings.
I like the clouds.
I fly down to the grass to eat it.
What am I?

Answer: A unicorn.

Isabelle Riley (5)
Greenfield Primary School, Countesthorpe

Jump

I can hop very high.
I hate foxes.
I like eating carrots.
I jump very high.
I live in a run.
You can keep me as a pet.
What am I?

Answer: A rabbit.

Aidan Gradden (5)
Greenfield Primary School, Countesthorpe

Eight Fuzzy Legs

I have eight fuzzy legs.
I like to build webs
and sometimes I can be scary.
I may live in your shed.
I like to eat flies.
What am I?

Answer: A spider.

Sebastian Goddard (7)
Greenfield Primary School, Countesthorpe

Purr-Fect Pet

I am a milk drinker.
I have whiskers.
I am fluffy.
I miaow to say please.
I purr when you stroke me.
I have four legs.
What am I?

Answer: A cat.

Mollie Edwards (5)
Greenfield Primary School, Countesthorpe

Tail Wagger

I have a tail.
I am black and white.
I like two walks a day.
I like to sleep and play.
I don't like the postman.
Who am I?

Answer: Alfie the dog.

Maisie Howett (7)
Greenfield Primary School, Countesthorpe

The High Hopper

I like to hop high
so I can catch the sun.
I like carrots and eating grass.
I can be a pet.
I am white, grey or black.
What am I?

Answer: A rabbit.

Evie Hunt (6)
Greenfield Primary School, Countesthorpe

What Am I?

I can fly in the sky really, really high.
I have big wings.
They open wide
so that in the air I can glide, really high.
What am I?

Answer: An eagle.

Reuben Hill (6)
Greenfield Primary School, Countesthorpe

Bark

I have a waggly tail.
I chew a bone.
I am your friend.
You can walk me on a lead.
I chase cats.
I like digging.
What am I?

Answer: A dog.

Josie Brant (6)
Greenfield Primary School, Countesthorpe

Never Forget

I have four legs.
I have a tail.
I have a trunk.
I have a big body.
I have a good memory.
I am grey.
What am I?

Answer: An elephant.

Teddie Atkins (5)
Greenfield Primary School, Countesthorpe

Flutter

I can fly.
I have wings.
I am pretty.
I am cute.
I am gorgeous.
I have antennae.
I am small.
What am I?

Answer: A butterfly.

Matilda Wright (6)
Greenfield Primary School, Countesthorpe

Feline Friend

I chase dogs.
I like milk.
I eat mice.
I have four legs.
I chase mice
and I say this... *Miaow!*
What am I?

Answer: A cat.

Max Shilton (6)
Greenfield Primary School, Countesthorpe

Speedy Speeder

I live in the jungle.
I eat meat.
I have strong jaws.
I have powerful legs.
I can run 100 miles an hour.
What am I?

Answer: A cheetah.

Alexandra Dowling (6)
Greenfield Primary School, Countesthorpe

The Flipper

I live in the ocean.
I have a flipper.
I am blue.
I am large.
I bob up and down.
I have a blow hole.
What am I?

Answer: A whale.

Isla Blossom Paragreen (6)
Greenfield Primary School, Countesthorpe

Imaginary Animal

I have wings.
I have a mane.
I have a tail.
I live on a rainbow.
I am in stories.
I have a horn.
What am I?

Answer: A unicorn.

Isabel Lewington (6)
Greenfield Primary School, Countesthorpe

Has A Horned Grey Head

I am as grey as a cloud.
I have two horns.
I have a tail.
I am big.
I am hunted.
I have four legs.
What am I?

Answer: A rhino.

Daniel John Bettles (6)
Greenfield Primary School, Countesthorpe

A Classroom Object

I have mud on me.
I'm made of fabric.
You can wear me.
I can be any colour.
You wear me on your feet.
What am I?

Answer: Shoes.

Isaac Lawrence (6)
Greenfield Primary School, Countesthorpe

Roar

I have stripes.
I like to roar and growl.
I like to fight.
I like to eat.
I have a long, stripy tail.
What am I?

Answer: A tiger.

Archie Underwood (5)
Greenfield Primary School, Countesthorpe

A Classroom Object

I can go through it.
I sometimes have windows on me.
I have a handle on me.
Sometimes I have a fire exit.
What am I?

Answer: A door.

Isla Sammels (5)
Greenfield Primary School, Countesthorpe

Cuddly Friend

I drink water.
I chase cats.
I like treats.
I live in your house.
I eat food.
I have four legs.
What am I?

Answer: A dog.

Austin Toby Worth (6)
Greenfield Primary School, Countesthorpe

Jumbo

I am grey.
I live in the wild.
I have a trunk.
I run.
I bath in a lake.
I have big ears.
What am I?

Answer: An elephant.

Imogen Ellen Worth (5)
Greenfield Primary School, Countesthorpe

The Sprayer

I have long ears.
I have a long trunk.
I have four legs.
I drink water.
I live in the jungle.
What am I?

Answer: An elephant.

Jessica Burniston (5)
Greenfield Primary School, Countesthorpe

Underground

I live underground.
I have a tail.
I have an orange body.
I have red eyes.
I am sly.
I sniff.
What am I?

Answer: A fox.

Luna Stevenson (6)
Greenfield Primary School, Countesthorpe

Yummy Biscuits

We are on TV.
We have a tasty house.
We have a bouncy bed.
We are a tasty family.
What are we?

Answer: The gingerbread family.

Kallum Beacham (5)
Greenfield Primary School, Countesthorpe

Horny Bla Bla Bla

I live in Alaska.
I have a thick nose.
I eat plants.
I have horns.
I have a beak.
What am I?

Answer: A pachyrhinosaurus.

Thomas Hollins (6)
Greenfield Primary School, Countesthorpe

You Can't Catch Me!

I am really fast.
I am tasty.
I don't like foxes.
I am a man but I'm not real.
What am I?

Answer: A gingerbread man.

Stanley Tyers (6)
Greenfield Primary School, Countesthorpe

Run Around

One of my favourite things
Is to run around the park
If I am unhappy
Then you might hear me bark
What am I?

·bop ∀ :ɹǝʍsu∀

Ruby Thompson (6)
Greenfield Primary School, Countesthorpe

Flying In The Sky

I am colourful.
I can fly.
I used to be a caterpillar.
I have wings.
I am pretty.
What am I?

Answer: A butterfly.

Jessica-Lily Jones (6)
Greenfield Primary School, Countesthorpe

I Have A Tail

I have a tail.
I like fish.
I have ears.
I have legs.
I can climb.
I like people.
What am I?

Answer: A cat.

Sophie Fox (6)
Greenfield Primary School, Countesthorpe

Trumpet Player?

I have long ears.
I am huge.
I have four legs.
I spray water.
I have a trunk.
What am I?

Answer: An elephant.

Darcie Booton (5)
Greenfield Primary School, Countesthorpe

A Classroom Object

I have numbers on me.
I am plastic.
I can help with drawing lines.
I am straight.
What am I?

Answer: A ruler.

Jude Clift (6)
Greenfield Primary School, Countesthorpe

Poisonous Pet

I have no legs.
I slither in the forest.
I hiss.
I am fast.
I spit venom.
What am I?

Answer: A snake.

Freddie Shilcock (6)
Greenfield Primary School, Countesthorpe

A Classroom Object

I can help you write.
I am red.
I am made out of wood.
You can rub me out.
What am I?

Answer: A pencil.

Taiyon Rhamell James Henry (6)
Greenfield Primary School, Countesthorpe

A Classroom Object

I have four legs.
I have black legs.
I have a red back.
You can sit on me.
What am I?

Answer: A chair.

Lucas Young (6)
Greenfield Primary School, Countesthorpe

A Classroom Object

I am big.
I go up to thirty.
I am plastic.
I'm used to draw lines.
What am I?

Answer: A ruler.

Lily Rose Illston-Hughes (5)
Greenfield Primary School, Countesthorpe

A Classroom Object

I have four legs.
I am red.
I am made of plastic.
You can sit on me.
What am I?

Answer: A chair.

Harry James Butler (6)
Greenfield Primary School, Countesthorpe

A Classroom Object

I live in the classroom.
I have four legs.
I am heavy.
I am red.
What am I?

Answer: A table.

Isobel Richardson (5)
Greenfield Primary School, Countesthorpe

A Classroom Object

I live in a pencil pot.
I can show numbers.
I go up to thirty.
What am I?

Answer: A number line.

Liam Blackett (6)
Greenfield Primary School, Countesthorpe

Long Distance Mover

I have lots of wheels.
I travel around the world.
I deliver cargo.
What am I?

Answer: A lorry.

James Toon (6)
Greenfield Primary School, Countesthorpe

A Classroom Object

I am on wheels.
I move around.
You sit on me.
I am black.
What am I?

Answer: A chair.

Giovanni Backus (5)
Greenfield Primary School, Countesthorpe

A Classroom Object

I can open.
I am big.
I have a window.
I have a handle.
What am I?

Answer: A door.

India Griffiths-Brown (6)
Greenfield Primary School, Countesthorpe

Doesn't Play Fairly

I am a big cat.
I live in hot countries.
I have spots.
What am I?

Answer: A cheetah.

Hiro Vine Peake (5)

Greenfield Primary School, Countesthorpe

Explosive Fun

I am noisy.
I can fly.
You see me on Bonfire Night.
What am I?

Answer: A rocket.

Dean Beacham (5)
Greenfield Primary School, Countesthorpe

Reaching The Stars

With others I share
But always fair.
Near or far
I keep in my heart.
The kindest one
Is to me.
Reaching the stars
Her love can be.
Who is she?

Answer: My mum.

Saeed Nurmamade (6)
Leicester International School, Leicester

Fun Time

I am cold.
I am white.
I have a round head.
I have a round body.
I melt in the sun.
You can make me when it snows.
What am I?

Answer: A snowman.

Fatemah Esat (6)
Leicester International School, Leicester

The Trees

My answer is...
Something that is hairy,
But don't worry, it's not scary.
They climb trees
But don't have wobbly knees.
They eat nuts
And don't share!
What is it?

Answer: A squirrel.

Deep Desai (5)
Manor House School, Ashby-De-La-Zouch

Inky

My answer is...
Something that is filled with ink.
I bet you can't find the missing link.
It has so many arms,
I bet it could set off hundreds of alarms.
What is it?

Answer: An octopus.

Samuel Gobey (5)
Manor House School, Ashby-De-La-Zouch

Falling On The Snow

My answer is...
Something that is cold
But doesn't get old.
It sparkles and shines
As it lands on the ground.
What is it?

Answer: A snowflake.

Zara Esat (6)
Manor House School, Ashby-De-La-Zouch

What Am I?

My answer is...
Something that you can eat.
I am made of a piece of meat
I have feathers instead of leather.
What am I?

Answer: A chicken.

Charlie Simon Dunn (6)
Manor House School, Ashby-De-La-Zouch

Frozen

My answer is...
Something that is cold
But never gets old.
Children build me.
I fill them with glee.
What am I?

Answer: A snowman.

Christopher Cheneler (6)
Manor House School, Ashby-De-La-Zouch

What Am I?

I love to lie on a furry rug
and I have triangle ears.
When I stay upstairs I lie down on a rug
and I am stripy.
I have pointy claws and four legs.
I have a lot of fur
and I don't like water or baths.
I have three claws on each paw
and I have twelve nails altogether.
What am I?

Answer: A cat.

Lexi-Rae Jordan-Summer (6)
Marriott Primary School, Leicester

What Am I?

I have long whiskers
and I have a lot of patterns.
I sit in the corner when I have babies.
I like to play outside with dogs
and I like to play ball.
I have big ears so I can hear a lot.
I climb up trees when I'm scared and I run.
What am I?

Answer: A cat.

Alfie Shenton (7)
Marriott Primary School, Leicester

What Am I?

I love to swing on the trees
and play at night with my friends.
When I have my dinner
it always tastes nice.
I sleep in the day
and play at night.
I have two little eyes
and two little legs.
What am I?

Answer: A bat.

Beau Noon (7)
Marriott Primary School, Leicester

What Am I?

I have furry fur.
I love to eat.
When someone strokes me I purr.
I have sharp and razor claws.
I am cute.
Sometimes I am soft.
What am I?

Answer: A cat.

Jack David Briers (7)
Marriott Primary School, Leicester

What Am I?

I live in a warm house.
I like to eat meat.
I have whiskers.
I am the colour ginger.
I like to drink milk.
I have soft ears.
What am I?

Answer: A cat.

Ifunanya Sophia Mbolu (7)
Marriott Primary School, Leicester

What Am I?

I have soft ears.
I have three whiskers.
I have three baby cats.
I have four legs.
I have a furry tail.
I have a home.
What am I?

Answer: A cat.

Nevaeh Feral (7)
Marriott Primary School, Leicester

What Am I?

I have pointy feet.
I fly at night.
When I fly I feel happy.
I love hanging up on the tree.
I like to eat fruit.
What am I?

Answer: A bat.

Sarah Pegararo (7)
Marriott Primary School, Leicester

What Am I?

I have four legs.
I have whiskers.
I have fur.
I like to sleep.
I have a long tail.
I live in a house.
What am I?

Answer: A cat.

Mia Alyssia Mayers (6)
Marriott Primary School, Leicester

What Am I?

I hiss.
I eat meat.
I am poisonous.
I don't make noise.
I like to sleep.
I am long and thin.
What am I?

Answer: A snake.

Jacek Machajewski (7)
Marriott Primary School, Leicester

What Am I?

I have a long body.
I have a fat face.
I have a long tongue.
I don't make a sound at night-time.
What am I?

Answer: A snake.

Tyler West (7)
Marriott Primary School, Leicester

What Am I?

I have four legs.
I have two eyes.
I eat sardines.
I drink milk or water.
I have fur.
What am I?

Answer: A cat.

Nicole Serwaa Antwi (7)
Marriott Primary School, Leicester

What Am I?

I eat meat.
I look like rope.
I'm good at hiding
and don't make noise.
What am I?

Answer: A snake.

Iyvvorie Smith (7)
Marriott Primary School, Leicester

What Am I?

I squeak in the dark.
I have long wings.
I have short legs.
I hang upside down.
What am I?

Answer: A bat.

Casey Crewe (7)
Marriott Primary School, Leicester

My Animal Riddle

My name begins with 's'.
I eat insects like worms and flies.
I live in a deep forest.
I have a red tongue like a slide.
I have a poisonous nose so don't touch me.
I don't have any legs or hands.
I am not a human, I am an animal.
I don't have sharp teeth.
I don't have wings to fly.
I can climb trees.
I live in leaves.
What am I?

Answer: A snake.

Juned Mulla (6)
Shenton Primary School, Leicester

My Animal Riddle

I can be yellow, white or spotty.
I nibble my food very quickly.
I am as cuddly as a cotton pillow.
I love to run around.
I have enormous teeth.
I have fluffy claws.
I have tall whiskers.
What am I?

Answer: A hamster.

Khadijha Yusuf (6)
Shenton Primary School, Leicester

I Like Pink

I have a long, pink body.
My body is only pink.
I don't have any hair.
I have a family
and my babies like to drink my milk.
I like to play in mud.
I have a curly tail and a round nose.
What am I?

Answer: A pig.

Darpan Barad (7)
Shenton Primary School, Leicester

Forest Animals

I have got black spots on my body.
I fight lions, tigers and other animals.
I hunt for meat.
I live in a wild jungle.
I have a long, wiggly tail.
I can run as fast as a motorbike.
What am I?

Answer: A cheetah.

Bilal Sajid (8)
Shenton Primary School, Leicester

Spindly Legs

I live in long, bushy fields.
My body is green and thin
like a twig.
I eat small flies.
I have long, spindly legs.
You can see me in summer.
I am very good at jumping.
What am I?

Answer: A grasshopper.

Rashan Al-Jaf (7)
Shenton Primary School, Leicester

My Animal Riddle

My animal has a white and black body.
My animal eats yummy fish from the sea.
My animal has orange wings.
It lives in the cold, freezing snow.
My animal looks after her babies.
What is it?

Answer: A penguin.

Navya Bharat Kumar (8)
Shenton Primary School, Leicester

What Is It?

My animal has four short legs
so it can run faster.
In the night my animal comes out
to hunt for its predator.
Its fur is softer than a cloud.
It's faster than a jackal.
What is it?

Answer: A fox.

Abdulaziz Fadra (6)
Shenton Primary School, Leicester

Swing Like A Monkey

I like to swing in trees.
I have sharp claws.
I have a little head.
You can see me in dark, wild forests.
I have sharp teeth.
I am fluffy like a dog.
I run slowly.
What am I?

Answer: A sloth.

Joy Patel (7)
Shenton Primary School, Leicester

What Is It?

My animal has slimy skin
and it can poison you.
It lives in the green jungle
and it comes out at night.
It can slither slowly.
It makes this sound... *Ssss!*
What is it?

Answer: A snake.

Abdirahman Iraad Saleeman (7)
Shenton Primary School, Leicester

My Long Legs

I have eight legs.
I have a fat head.
I catch my food in the water.
I like to wiggle my eight legs.
I go fast.
I live in the ocean.
I like to eat fish.
What am I?

Answer: An octopus.

Noelkanth Naresh (7)
Shenton Primary School, Leicester

Fright

I come out at night.
I give you a big fright.
I do not like daylight.
I might give you a vampire bite.
I can fly higher than a kite.
I am very light.
What am I?

Answer: A bat.

Aayan Shaik (7)
Shenton Primary School, Leicester

Pink Stink

My skin is pink.
I have a small, twirly tail.
I have small ears.
I have tiny, small, black eyes.
I have four small legs.
I have a round, flat nose.
What am I?

Answer: A pig.

Shafeeqah Taylar (6)
Shenton Primary School, Leicester

My Animal Riddle

My animal has short legs
so it hunts fast.
It lives in the deep, creaky forest.
Its fur is orange and white
like a tiger.
This animal dashes fast.
What is it?

Answer: A fox.

Dhriti Natubhai (7)
Shenton Primary School, Leicester

Appearance

I can loudly growl.
I am brown.
I am a fabulous noun.
I'm also black.
I'm bigger than an ugly sack.
If I go, I'm not coming back!
What am I?

Answer: A bear.

Khadijah Farah (6)
Shenton Primary School, Leicester

Fierce

I have no fur.
I slither on the ground.
You can find me in a jungle.
I can poison you.
I have very sharp fangs
and I am a reptile.
What am I?

Answer: An anaconda.

Muhammad Sarang (7)
Shenton Primary School, Leicester

I Swim In The Water

I have a shell and I walk with it everywhere.
I have small, black eyes.
I have four short legs.
I have a rocky body.
My shell is hard.
What am I?

Answer: A turtle.

Azraa Pira (7)
Shenton Primary School, Leicester

I Like Bananas

I live in the zoo.
I can eat bananas.
I can say 'oooo'.
I have my family.
I can swing on the rope.
I can be angry.
What am I?

Answer: A monkey.

Hamza Geedi (7)
Shenton Primary School, Leicester

I Have Stripes

I have stripes.
I have a long, thin body.
I leave slimy tracks.
I love water.
I swim in the water.
I don't have legs.
What am I?

Answer: A snake.

Aaryan Patel (6)
Shenton Primary School, Leicester

My Animal Riddle

My animal has short legs to dash.
I live in the deep forest.
In the night I quietly come out of the forest.
You can't touch me.
What am I?

Answer: A fox.

Muhammad Bahadur (6)
Shenton Primary School, Leicester

Slow Coach

I am slow.
I like to go on trees.
I can climb up trees.
I am fluffy and soft.
I am a slowcoach.
I am grey.
What am I?

Answer: A sloth.

Sumaya Latifah (6)
Shenton Primary School, Leicester

Insect Catcher

I have pointy, sharp, little nails.
I eat bugs with my long tongue.
I walk around looking for bugs.
What am I?

Answer: A lizard.

Humairaa Khalifa (6)
Shenton Primary School, Leicester

Young**Writers**
Est.1991

YOUNG WRITERS INFORMATION

We hope you have enjoyed reading this book – and that you will continue to in the coming years.

If you're a young writer who enjoys reading and creative writing, or the parent of an enthusiastic poet or story writer, do visit our website **www.youngwriters.co.uk**. Here you will find free competitions, workshops and games, as well as recommended reads, a poetry glossary and our blog.

If you would like to order further copies of this book, or any of our other titles, then please give us a call or visit **www.youngwriters.co.uk**.

Young Writers
Remus House
Coltsfoot Drive
Peterborough
PE2 9BF
(01733) 890066
info@youngwriters.co.uk